LITTLE BLACK

CASINO BOOK

This little black book belongs to:

O——————————————————O

DATE: ○————————○

CITY: ○————————○

PROPERTY: ○————————○

DAY'S FINAL RESULTS   UP

$

                    DOWN

$

$ DAILY BUDGET

$

$ AT END OF DAY

$

NOTES:

BIG WINS

$ ●

$ ●

$ ●

4

DATE: o———————o

CITY: o———————o

PROPERTY: o———————o

DAY'S FINAL RESULTS

UP

$

DOWN

$

$ DAILY BUDGET

$

$ AT END OF DAY

$

NOTES:

BIG WINS

$ ———————•

$ ———————•

$ ———————•

DATE: o———————o

CITY: o———————o

PROPERTY: o———————o

DAY'S FINAL RESULTS

UP

$

DOWN

$

$ DAILY BUDGET

$

$ AT END OF DAY

$

NOTES:

BIG WINS

$ ———————●

$ ———————●

$ ———————●

DATE: o————————o
CITY: o————————o
PROPERTY: o————————o

DAY'S FINAL RESULTS

UP $

DOWN $

$ DAILY BUDGET

$

$ AT END OF DAY

$

NOTES:

BIG WINS

$ ————————•
$ ————————•
$ ————————•

DATE: o———————o

CITY: o———————o

PROPERTY: o———————o

DAY'S FINAL RESULTS

$ UP

$ DOWN

$ DAILY BUDGET

$

$ AT END OF DAY

$

NOTES:

BIG WINS

$ ———————●

$ ———————●

$ ———————●

DATE: o————————o

CITY: o————————o

PROPERTY: o————————o

DAY'S FINAL RESULTS

UP

$

DOWN

$

$ DAILY BUDGET

$

$ AT END OF DAY

$

NOTES:

BIG WINS

$ ———o

$ ———o

$ ———o

DATE: o————————o

CITY: o————————o

PROPERTY: o————————o

DAY'S FINAL RESULTS   UP

($)

                                      DOWN

                        ($)

$ DAILY BUDGET

($)

            $ AT END OF DAY

                  ($)

NOTES:

                              BIG WINS

                        ($)————————●

                        ($)————————●

                        ($)————————●

DATE: ○————————○

CITY: ○————————○

PROPERTY: ○————————○

DAY'S FINAL RESULTS

UP

($)

DOWN

($)

$ DAILY BUDGET

($)

$ AT END OF DAY

($)

NOTES:

BIG WINS

($)————●

($)————●

($)————●

DATE: o————————o

CITY: o————————o

PROPERTY: o————————o

DAY'S FINAL RESULTS

UP

$

DOWN

$

$ DAILY BUDGET

$

$ AT END OF DAY

$

NOTES:

BIG WINS

$ ————————•

$ ————————•

$ ————————•

DATE: o————————o

CITY: o————————o

PROPERTY: o————————o

DAY'S FINAL RESULTS

UP

($)

DOWN

($)

$ DAILY BUDGET

($)

$ AT END OF DAY

($)

NOTES:

BIG WINS

($) ————●

($) ————●

($) ————●

DATE: ○————————○
CITY: ○————————○
PROPERTY: ○————————○

DAY'S FINAL RESULTS   UP

$

DOWN

$

$ DAILY BUDGET

$

$ AT END OF DAY

$

NOTES:

BIG WINS

$ ————————●
$ ————————●
$ ————————●

DATE: o———————o

CITY: o———————o

PROPERTY: o———————o

DAY'S FINAL RESULTS   UP

$

DOWN

$

$ DAILY BUDGET

$

$ AT END OF DAY

$

NOTES:

BIG WINS

$ •———————•

$ •———————•

$ •———————•

DATE: ○————————————○

CITY: ○————————————○

PROPERTY: ○————————————○

DAY'S FINAL RESULTS

$ UP

DOWN

$ DAILY BUDGET

$

$ AT END OF DAY

$

NOTES:

BIG WINS

$ ————————●

$ ————————●

$ ————————●

DATE: o————————o
CITY: o————————o
PROPERTY: o————————o

DAY'S FINAL RESULTS

UP

$

DOWN

$

$ DAILY BUDGET

$

$ AT END OF DAY

$

NOTES:

BIG WINS

$ ————————•
$ ————————•
$ ————————•

DATE: ○————————————○
CITY: ○————————————○
PROPERTY: ○————————————○

DAY'S FINAL RESULTS

UP

$

DOWN

$ DAILY BUDGET

$

$ AT END OF DAY

$

NOTES:

$

BIG WINS

$ ————————●
$ ————————●
$ ————————●

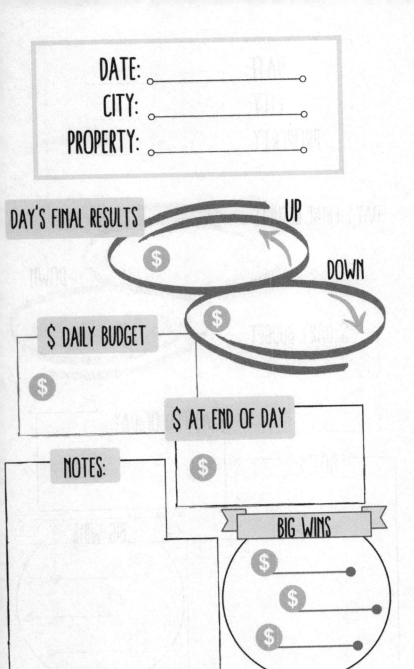

DATE:

CITY:

PROPERTY:

DAY'S FINAL RESULTS

UP

DOWN

$ DAILY BUDGET

$ AT END OF DAY

NOTES:

BIG WINS

19

DATE: ○————————○
CITY: ○————————○
PROPERTY: ○————————○

DAY'S FINAL RESULTS

UP

$

DOWN

$

$ DAILY BUDGET

$

$ AT END OF DAY

$

NOTES:

BIG WINS

$
$
$

DATE: o———————o
CITY: o———————o
PROPERTY: o———————o

DAY'S FINAL RESULTS

UP

$

DOWN

$

$ DAILY BUDGET

$

$ AT END OF DAY

$

NOTES:

BIG WINS

$ ————o

$ ————o

$ ————o

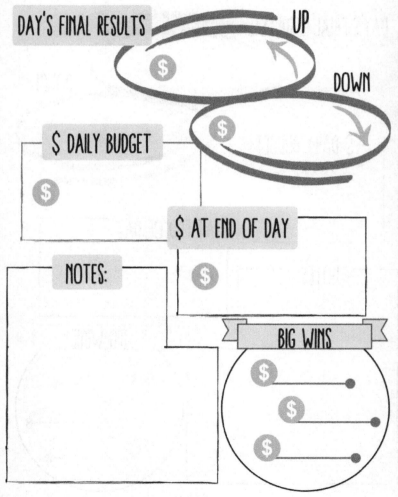

DATE: ○——————○

CITY: ○——————○

PROPERTY: ○——————○

DAY'S FINAL RESULTS

UP

DOWN

$ DAILY BUDGET

$ AT END OF DAY

NOTES:

BIG WINS

DATE: _____

CITY: _____

PROPERTY: _____

DAY'S FINAL RESULTS

UP

DOWN

$

$

$ DAILY BUDGET

$

$ AT END OF DAY

$

NOTES:

BIG WINS

$ _____●

$ _____●

$ _____●

DATE: o———————o

CITY: o———————o

PROPERTY: o———————o

DAY'S FINAL RESULTS

UP

$

DOWN

$

$ DAILY BUDGET

$

$ AT END OF DAY

$

NOTES:

BIG WINS

$ ———————●

$ ———————●

$ ———————●

DATE: ○————————————○
CITY: ○————————————○
PROPERTY: ○————————————○

DAY'S FINAL RESULTS

UP

($)

DOWN

$ DAILY BUDGET

($)

$ AT END OF DAY

($)

NOTES:

BIG WINS

($)————————●
($)————————●
($)————————●

DATE: o———————o

CITY: o———————o

PROPERTY: o———————o

DAY'S FINAL RESULTS

UP

$

DOWN

$ DAILY BUDGET

$

$

$ AT END OF DAY

$

NOTES:

BIG WINS

$ ————————•

$ ————————•

$ ————————•

DATE: ○———————○

CITY: ○———————○

PROPERTY: ○———————○

DAY'S FINAL RESULTS

UP

$

DOWN

$

$ DAILY BUDGET

$

$ AT END OF DAY

$

NOTES:

BIG WINS

$ ●————●

$ ●————●

$ ●————●

DATE: o————————o

CITY: o————————o

PROPERTY: o————————o

DAY'S FINAL RESULTS

UP

$

DOWN

$

$ DAILY BUDGET

$

$ AT END OF DAY

$

NOTES:

BIG WINS

$ ————●

$ ————●

$ ————●

DATE: o————————o

CITY: o————————o

PROPERTY: o————————o

DAY'S FINAL RESULTS

UP

$

DOWN

$ DAILY BUDGET

$

$ AT END OF DAY

$

NOTES:

BIG WINS

$ ———————●

$ ———————●

$ ———————●

DATE: ○————————○
CITY: ○————————○
PROPERTY: ○————————○

DAY'S FINAL RESULTS

UP

($)

DOWN

$ DAILY BUDGET

($)

$ AT END OF DAY

($)

NOTES:

BIG WINS

($)———●
($)———●
($)———●

DATE: ○————————○
CITY: ○————————○
PROPERTY: ○————————○

DAY'S FINAL RESULTS

UP

$

DOWN

$

$ DAILY BUDGET

$

$ AT END OF DAY

$

NOTES:

BIG WINS

$ ————————●

$ ————————●

$ ————————●

DATE: o———————o

CITY: o———————o

PROPERTY: o———————o

DAY'S FINAL RESULTS   UP

$

DOWN

$

$ DAILY BUDGET

$

$ AT END OF DAY

$

NOTES:

BIG WINS

$ ———————•

$ ———————•

$ ———————•

DATE: ○———————○
CITY: ○———————○
PROPERTY: ○———————○

DAY'S FINAL RESULTS

UP

$

DOWN

$

$ DAILY BUDGET

$

$ AT END OF DAY

$

NOTES:

BIG WINS

$ ●——————●
$ ●——————●
$ ●——————●

DATE: o————o

CITY: o————o

PROPERTY: o————o

DAY'S FINAL RESULTS

UP

$

DOWN

$ DAILY BUDGET

$

$

$ AT END OF DAY

$

NOTES:

BIG WINS

$ ————•

$ ————•

$ ————•

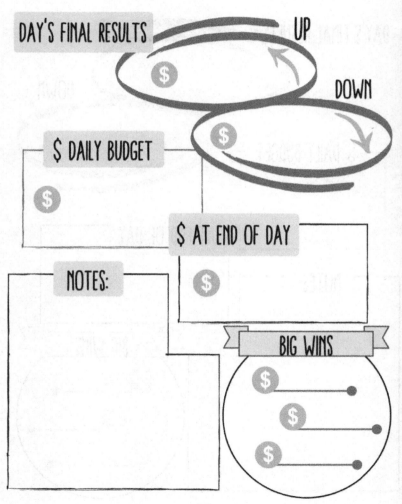

DATE: o————————o

CITY: o————————o

PROPERTY: o————————o

DAY'S FINAL RESULTS

UP

$

DOWN

$

$ DAILY BUDGET

$

$ AT END OF DAY

$

NOTES:

BIG WINS

$ ———————•

$ ———————•

$ ———————•

DATE: o——————o

CITY: o——————o

PROPERTY: o——————o

DAY'S FINAL RESULTS

UP

DOWN

$

$

$ DAILY BUDGET

$

$ AT END OF DAY

$

NOTES:

BIG WINS

$ ————o

$ ————o

$ ————o

DATE: _____
CITY: _____
PROPERTY: _____

DAY'S FINAL RESULTS

UP

$

DOWN

$ DAILY BUDGET

$

$

$ AT END OF DAY

$

NOTES:

BIG WINS

$ _____
$ _____
$ _____

DATE: o————————o

CITY: o————————o

PROPERTY: o————————o

DAY'S FINAL RESULTS

UP

DOWN

$

$

$ DAILY BUDGET

$

$ AT END OF DAY

$

NOTES:

BIG WINS

$

$

$

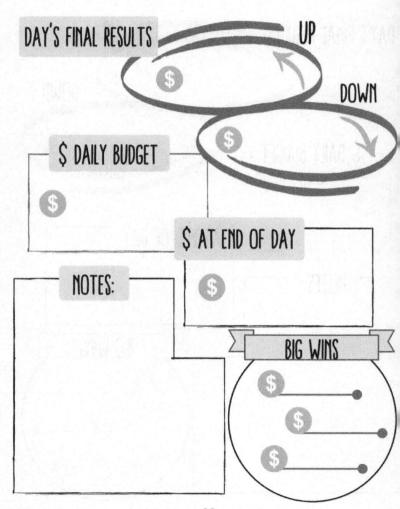

DATE: ○————————————○
CITY: ○————————————○
PROPERTY: ○————————————○

DAY'S FINAL RESULTS

UP

($)

DOWN

$ DAILY BUDGET

($)

$ AT END OF DAY

($)

NOTES:

BIG WINS

($)————————●
($)————————●
($)————————●

DATE: ○————————○

CITY: ○————————○

PROPERTY: ○————————○

DAY'S FINAL RESULTS

UP

$

DOWN

$

$ DAILY BUDGET

$

$ AT END OF DAY

$

NOTES:

BIG WINS

$ ————●

$ ————●

$ ————●

DATE: ○————————○

CITY: ○————————○

PROPERTY: ○————————○

DAY'S FINAL RESULTS

UP

$

DOWN

$

$ DAILY BUDGET

$

$ AT END OF DAY

$

NOTES:

BIG WINS

$ ——————●

$ ——————●

$ ——————●

DATE: o————————o

CITY: o————————o

PROPERTY: o————————o

DAY'S FINAL RESULTS

UP

$

DOWN

$

$ DAILY BUDGET

$

$ AT END OF DAY

$

NOTES:

BIG WINS

$ ————————•

$ ————————•

$ ————————•

DATE: o————————o
CITY: o————————o
PROPERTY: o————————o

DAY'S FINAL RESULTS

UP

$

DOWN

$

$ DAILY BUDGET

$

$ AT END OF DAY

$

NOTES:

BIG WINS

$ ————•

$ ————•

$ ————•

43

DATE: o————————o
CITY: o————————o
PROPERTY: o————————o

DAY'S FINAL RESULTS

UP

$

DOWN

$ DAILY BUDGET

$

$ AT END OF DAY

$

NOTES:

BIG WINS

$ ————●
$ ————●
$ ————●

DATE: _____

CITY: _____

PROPERTY: _____

DAY'S FINAL RESULTS

UP

$

DOWN

$

$ DAILY BUDGET

$

$ AT END OF DAY

$

NOTES:

BIG WINS

$ _____

$ _____

$ _____

DATE: ○─────────○
CITY: ○─────────○
PROPERTY: ○─────────○

DAY'S FINAL RESULTS

UP

$

DOWN

$ DAILY BUDGET

$

$ AT END OF DAY

$

NOTES:

$

BIG WINS

$ ●
$ ●
$ ●

DATE: ○——————○

CITY: ○——————○

PROPERTY: ○——————○

DAY'S FINAL RESULTS

UP

$

DOWN

$

$ DAILY BUDGET

$

$ AT END OF DAY

$

NOTES:

BIG WINS

$ ——————●

$ ——————●

$ ——————●

DATE: ○————————○

CITY: ○————————○

PROPERTY: ○————————○

DAY'S FINAL RESULTS

UP

$

DOWN

$

$ DAILY BUDGET

$

$ AT END OF DAY

$

NOTES:

BIG WINS

$ ————————●

$ ————————●

$ ————————●

DATE: o————————o

CITY: o————————o

PROPERTY: o————————o

DAY'S FINAL RESULTS

UP

$

DOWN

$

$ DAILY BUDGET

$

$ AT END OF DAY

$

NOTES:

BIG WINS

$ ————————•

$ ————————•

$ ————————•

DATE: o_____o

CITY: o_____o

PROPERTY: o_____o

DAY'S FINAL RESULTS   UP

$

DOWN

$ DAILY BUDGET

$

$ AT END OF DAY

$

NOTES:

BIG WINS

$_____•

$_____•

$_____•

DATE: o————————o

CITY: o————————o

PROPERTY: o————————o

DAY'S FINAL RESULTS

UP

$

DOWN

$

$ DAILY BUDGET

$

$ AT END OF DAY

$

NOTES:

BIG WINS

$ ————•

$ ————•

$ ————•

DATE: o———————o

CITY: o———————o

PROPERTY: o———————o

DAY'S FINAL RESULTS

UP

$

DOWN

$

$ DAILY BUDGET

$

$ AT END OF DAY

$

NOTES:

BIG WINS

$ ———————●

$ ———————●

$ ———————●

DATE: ○————————○
CITY: ○————————○
PROPERTY: ○————————○

DAY'S FINAL RESULTS

UP

$

DOWN

$

$ DAILY BUDGET

$

$ AT END OF DAY

$

NOTES:

BIG WINS

$ ————————●

$ ————————●

$ ————————●

DATE: o————————o

CITY: o————————o

PROPERTY: o————————o

DAY'S FINAL RESULTS

$ UP

$ DOWN

$ DAILY BUDGET

$

$ AT END OF DAY

$

NOTES:

BIG WINS

$ ————•

$ ————•

$ ————•

DATE: o————————o
CITY: o————————o
PROPERTY: o————————o

DAY'S FINAL RESULTS

UP

$

DOWN

$

$ DAILY BUDGET

$

$ AT END OF DAY

$

NOTES:

BIG WINS

$ ————————•

$ ————————•

$ ————————•

DATE: o———————o

CITY: o———————o

PROPERTY: o———————o

DAY'S FINAL RESULTS

UP

$

DOWN

$ DAILY BUDGET

$

$ AT END OF DAY

$

NOTES:

BIG WINS

$ ———•

$ ———•

$ ———•

DATE: ○—————○

CITY: ○—————○

PROPERTY: ○—————○

DAY'S FINAL RESULTS

UP

$

DOWN

$

$ DAILY BUDGET

$

$ AT END OF DAY

$

NOTES:

BIG WINS

$ ————●

$ ————●

$ ————●

DATE: o———————o

CITY: o———————o

PROPERTY: o———————o

DAY'S FINAL RESULTS

UP

$

DOWN

$

$ DAILY BUDGET

$

$ AT END OF DAY

$

NOTES:

BIG WINS

$ ———●

$ ———●

$ ———●

DATE: ○————————○
CITY: ○————————○
PROPERTY: ○————————○

DAY'S FINAL RESULTS

UP

$

DOWN

$

$ DAILY BUDGET

$

$ AT END OF DAY

$

NOTES:

BIG WINS

$ ————————●
$ ————————●
$ ————————●

DATE: ○————————○

CITY: ○————————○

PROPERTY: ○————————○

DAY'S FINAL RESULTS

UP

$

DOWN

$

$ DAILY BUDGET

$

$ AT END OF DAY

$

NOTES:

BIG WINS

$ ————●

$ ————●

$ ————●

DATE: o_____o

CITY: o_____o

PROPERTY: o_____o

DAY'S FINAL RESULTS

UP

$

DOWN

$ DAILY BUDGET

$

$ AT END OF DAY

$

NOTES:

BIG WINS

$ _____•

$ _____•

$ _____•

61

DATE: o———————o

CITY: o———————o

PROPERTY: o———————o

DAY'S FINAL RESULTS

$

UP

$

DOWN

$ DAILY BUDGET

$

$ AT END OF DAY

$

NOTES:

BIG WINS

$ ———————●

$ ———————●

$ ———————●

DATE: ○————————○

CITY: ○————————○

PROPERTY: ○————————○

DAY'S FINAL RESULTS

UP

$

DOWN

$

$ DAILY BUDGET

$

$ AT END OF DAY

$

NOTES:

BIG WINS

$ ●————●

$ ●————●

$ ●————●

DATE: ○————————○

CITY: ○————————○

PROPERTY: ○————————○

DAY'S FINAL RESULTS

UP

($)

DOWN

($)

$ DAILY BUDGET

($)

$ AT END OF DAY

($)

NOTES:

BIG WINS

($) ————●

($) ————●

($) ————●

DATE: ○————————○
CITY: ○————————○
PROPERTY: ○————————○

DAY'S FINAL RESULTS

UP

DOWN

$

$

$ DAILY BUDGET

$

$ AT END OF DAY

$

NOTES:

BIG WINS

$ ————————●
$ ————————●
$ ————————●

DATE: ○————————————○

CITY: ○————————————○

PROPERTY: ○————————————○

DAY'S FINAL RESULTS   UP

($)

                    DOWN

                    ($)

$ DAILY BUDGET

($)

            $ AT END OF DAY

            ($)

NOTES:

                    BIG WINS

                    ($)————●

                        ($)————●

                    ($)————●

DATE: o———————o

CITY: o———————o

PROPERTY: o———————o

DAY'S FINAL RESULTS

$

UP

DOWN

$

$ DAILY BUDGET

$

$ AT END OF DAY

$

NOTES:

BIG WINS

$ ————•

$ ————•

$ ————•

DATE: o————————o

CITY: o————————o

PROPERTY: o————————o

DAY'S FINAL RESULTS

UP

$

DOWN

$

$ DAILY BUDGET

$

$ AT END OF DAY

$

NOTES:

BIG WINS

$ ————●

$ ————●

$ ————●

DATE: ○————————————○

CITY: ○————————————○

PROPERTY: ○————————————○

DAY'S FINAL RESULTS

UP

$

DOWN

$

$ DAILY BUDGET

$

$ AT END OF DAY

$

NOTES:

BIG WINS

$ ————————●

$ ————————●

$ ————————●

DATE: ○―――――――○
CITY: ○―――――――○
PROPERTY: ○―――――――○

DAY'S FINAL RESULTS

UP

$

DOWN

$ DAILY BUDGET

$

$ AT END OF DAY

$

NOTES:

BIG WINS

$ ――――●

$ ――――●

$ ――――●

DATE: o———————o

CITY: o———————o

PROPERTY: o———————o

DAY'S FINAL RESULTS

UP

$

DOWN

$

$ DAILY BUDGET

$

$ AT END OF DAY

$

NOTES:

BIG WINS

$ ————————•

$ ————————•

$ ————————•

DATE: o———o

CITY: o———o

PROPERTY: o———o

DAY'S FINAL RESULTS

UP

$

DOWN

$

$ DAILY BUDGET

$

$ AT END OF DAY

$

NOTES:

BIG WINS

$ ———•

$ ———•

$ ———•

DATE: o————————o
CITY: o————————o
PROPERTY: o————————o

DAY'S FINAL RESULTS

UP

($)

DOWN

($)

$ DAILY BUDGET

($)

$ AT END OF DAY

($)

NOTES:

BIG WINS

($) ————————•
($) ————————•
($) ————————•

DATE: o_____o

CITY: o_____o

PROPERTY: o_____o

DAY'S FINAL RESULTS   UP

$ DOWN

$ DAILY BUDGET

$

$ AT END OF DAY

$

NOTES:

BIG WINS

$ ●_____●

$ ●_____●

$ ●_____●

DATE: ○————————○

CITY: ○————————○

PROPERTY: ○————————○

DAY'S FINAL RESULTS

UP

$

DOWN

$

$ DAILY BUDGET

$

$ AT END OF DAY

$

NOTES:

BIG WINS

$ ————————●

$ ————————●

$ ————————●

DATE: ○————————○
CITY: ○————————○
PROPERTY: ○————————○

DAY'S FINAL RESULTS

UP

($)

DOWN

$ DAILY BUDGET

($)

$ AT END OF DAY

($)

NOTES:

BIG WINS

($)————●

($)————●

($)————●

DATE: ○———————○
CITY: ○———————○
PROPERTY: ○———————○

DAY'S FINAL RESULTS

UP

$

DOWN

$

$ DAILY BUDGET

$

$ AT END OF DAY

$

NOTES:

BIG WINS

$ ●
$ ●
$ ●

DATE: o————————o

CITY: o————————o

PROPERTY: o————————o

DAY'S FINAL RESULTS

UP

$

DOWN

$

$ DAILY BUDGET

$

$ AT END OF DAY

$

NOTES:

BIG WINS

$ ————●

$ ————●

$ ————●

DATE: o————————o

CITY: o————————o

PROPERTY: o————————o

DAY'S FINAL RESULTS

UP

($)

DOWN

($)

$ DAILY BUDGET

($)

$ AT END OF DAY

($)

NOTES:

BIG WINS

($)————————•

($)————————•

($)————————•

DATE: ○————————○

CITY: ○————————○

PROPERTY: ○————————○

DAY'S FINAL RESULTS

UP

$

DOWN

$

$ DAILY BUDGET

$

$ AT END OF DAY

$

NOTES:

BIG WINS

$ ————●

$ ————●

$ ————●

DATE: _____

CITY: _____

PROPERTY: _____

DAY'S FINAL RESULTS

$

UP

DOWN

$

$ DAILY BUDGET

$

$ AT END OF DAY

$

NOTES:

BIG WINS

$ _____

$ _____

$ _____

DATE: o—————o

CITY: o—————o

PROPERTY: o—————o

DAY'S FINAL RESULTS

UP

$

DOWN

$

$ DAILY BUDGET

$

$ AT END OF DAY

$

NOTES:

BIG WINS

$ ———o

$ ———o

$ ———o

DATE: ○————————○

CITY: ○————————○

PROPERTY: ○————————○

DAY'S FINAL RESULTS

UP

$

DOWN

$

$ DAILY BUDGET

$

$ AT END OF DAY

$

NOTES:

BIG WINS

$ ————————●

$ ————————●

$ ————————●

DATE: o———————o

CITY: o———————o

PROPERTY: o———————o

DAY'S FINAL RESULTS

$ UP

$ DOWN

$ DAILY BUDGET

$

$ AT END OF DAY

$

NOTES:

BIG WINS

$ ———————●

$ ———————●

$ ———————●

DATE: o————————o

CITY: o————————o

PROPERTY: o————————o

DAY'S FINAL RESULTS

UP

$

DOWN

$

$ DAILY BUDGET

$

$ AT END OF DAY

$

NOTES:

BIG WINS

$——————•

$——————•

$——————•

DATE: o———————o

CITY: o———————o

PROPERTY: o———————o

DAY'S FINAL RESULTS

UP

$

DOWN

$

$ DAILY BUDGET

$

$ AT END OF DAY

$

NOTES:

BIG WINS

$ ———————•

$ ———————•

$ ———————•

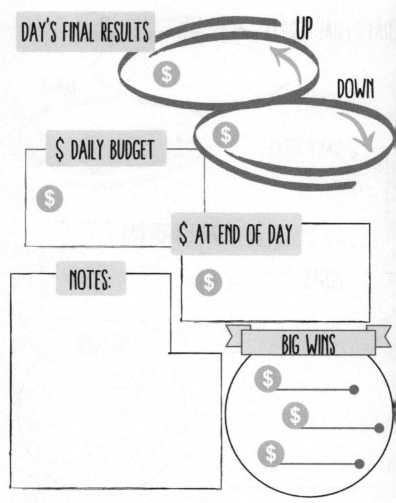

DATE: ○————————○

CITY: ○————————○

PROPERTY: ○————————○

DAY'S FINAL RESULTS

UP

$

DOWN

$

$ DAILY BUDGET

$

$ AT END OF DAY

$

NOTES:

BIG WINS

$ ———————●

$ ———————●

$ ———————●

DATE: ○————————○

CITY: ○————————○

PROPERTY: ○————————○

DAY'S FINAL RESULTS

UP

$

DOWN

$

$ DAILY BUDGET

$

$ AT END OF DAY

$

NOTES:

BIG WINS

$ ————●

$ ————●

$ ————●

DATE: ○——————○
CITY: ○——————○
PROPERTY: ○——————○

DAY'S FINAL RESULTS

UP

DOWN

$ DAILY BUDGET

$

$ AT END OF DAY

$

NOTES:

BIG WINS

$ ——————●
$ ——————●
$ ——————●

DATE: o———————o

CITY: o———————o

PROPERTY: o———————o

DAY'S FINAL RESULTS

$ UP

DOWN

$ DAILY BUDGET

$

$ AT END OF DAY

$

NOTES:

BIG WINS

$ ———●

$ ———●

$ ———●

DATE: o_____o

CITY: o_____o

PROPERTY: o_____o

DAY'S FINAL RESULTS

UP

($)

DOWN

$ DAILY BUDGET

($)

$ AT END OF DAY

($)

NOTES:

BIG WINS

($)———●

($)———●

($)———●

DATE: o————————o

CITY: o————————o

PROPERTY: o————————o

DAY'S FINAL RESULTS

UP

$

DOWN

$

$ DAILY BUDGET

$

$ AT END OF DAY

$

NOTES:

BIG WINS

$ ———•

$ ———•

$ ———•

DATE: ○————————○

CITY: ○————————○

PROPERTY: ○————————○

DAY'S FINAL RESULTS

UP

DOWN

$ DAILY BUDGET

$

$ AT END OF DAY

$

NOTES:

BIG WINS

$ ————————●

$ ————————●

$ ————————●

Time to reorder.

LITTLE BLACK CASINO BOOK

Date	City	Property	Pg. No.	+$Up/ -$Down

Index

Index				
Date	City	Property	Pg. No.	+$Up/ -$Down

Index

Date	City	Property	Pg. No.	+$Up/ -$Down

Date	City	Property	Pg. No.	+$Up/ -$Down

Index

Date	City	Property	Pg. No.	+$Up/ -$Down

Index

Index				
Date	City	Property	Pg. No.	+$Up/ -$Down

Made in United States
Orlando, FL
03 December 2024

54905070R00055